Simply Chenille Baby Quilts

It's no secret that babies who are showered with tender-loving care grow up happy and secure! So hold them close to your heart, swaddled in a cozy quilt made just for them. The six crib-size quilts in this collection are pieced using chenille, so they're extra soft and just right for snuggling! Little ones will love the warm, fluffy feel of the chenille against their tender skin — and moms' hearts will melt! Best of all, these sweet-and-simple designs can be made in a flash, so you'll have more time to spend cuddling your bundle of joy.

Bonnie Olaveson

What started out as a doll-making venture some 12 years ago has blossomed for Bonnie Olaveson. Her business, Cotton Way, has grown to include wearables, wall hangings, table runners, quilts, and clay buttons. They also make cotton rag for doll hair and rag quilts. Life events, such as graduations and weddings, inspire Bonnie's designs. The recent birth of her first grandchild, Britton, sparked her interest in designing baby quilts. Bonnie, who has been sewing since the age of 6, counts it a blessing to be able to have a job doing what she loves.

Rock-a-Bye Baby

This baby quilt is as easy to make as it is pretty. Blocks of cheery yellow print are alternated with white chenille to complete the fresh-as-spring design. For Baby's safety, take extra care in attaching the tiny lace doilies and silk ribbon roses. This dainty quilt also makes a sweet wall hanging for the nursery.

Block Size: 5" x 5" (13 x 13 cm)
Quilt Size: 46"x 46" (117 cm x 117 cm)

YARDAGE REQUIREMENTS
Yardage is based on 45"w fabric.

- ☐ 1 yd (91 cm) yellow print
- ☐ 1 yd (91 cm) white chenille
- 3 yds (2.7 m) for backing
- ¾ yd (69 cm) for binding
- 50" x 50" (127 x 127 cm) square of batting
- 40 3" (8cm) doilies (optional)
- 40 small silk ribbon rosebuds (optional)

CUTTING OUT THE PIECES
All measurements include a ¼" seam allowance.
Follow Rotary Cutting, page 16, to cut fabric.

1. From yellow print: ☐
   - Cut 6 strips 5½"w. From these strips, cut 40 **squares** 5½" x 5½".
2. From white chenille: ☐
   - Cut 6 strips 5½"w. From these strips, cut 41 **squares** 5½" x 5½".

ASSEMBLING THE QUILT TOP
Follow Piecing and Pressing, page 19, to make quilt top.

1. Center doilies on yellow squares and stitch in place. Sew rosebuds to center of doilies. **NOTE:** *Small objects can be a choking hazard for babies or small children. Make sure they are securely attached.*
2. Sew 5 white chenille **squares** and 4 yellow print **squares** together to make **Row A**. Make 5 **Row A's**.

Row A (make 5)

3. Sew 4 white chenille **squares** and 5 yellow print **squares** together to make **Row B**. Make 4 **Row B's**.

Row B (make 4)

4. Referring to photo, sew 5 **Row A's** and 4 **Row B's** together to complete quilt top.

COMPLETING THE QUILT
1. Follow **Quilting**, page 21, to mark, layer and quilt as desired. Our quilt is machine quilted "in the ditch".
2. Cut a 24" square of binding fabric. Follow **Binding**, page 25, to bind quilt using 2½"w bias binding with mitered corners.

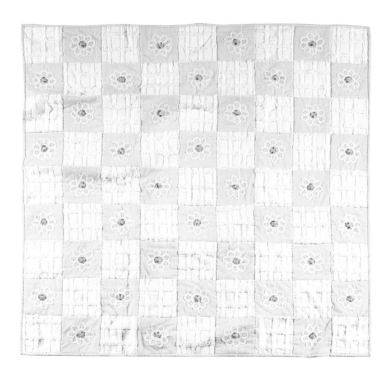

Roses & Bows

Babies grow up so quickly! Piece this Hourglass quilt as a reminder to not let time slip by without enjoying every minute. Offering a hint of femininity, pink floral squares complement the solid pink and white chenille Hourglass blocks. Silk ribbon roses complete the look, but be sure they're sewn on securely so your little princess can't "pick" the flowers.

Block Size: 5¼" x 5¼" (13 x 13 cm)
Quilt Size: 43"x 43" (109 cm x 109 cm)

YARDAGE REQUIREMENTS
Yardage is based on 45"w fabric.

- ☐ 1 yd (91 cm) pink floral
- ▨ ⅝ yd (57 cm) pink solid
- ☐ ⅝ yd (57 cm) white chenille
  2¾ yds (2.5 m) for backing
  ¾ yd (69 cm) for binding
  47" x 47" (119 x 119 cm) square of batting
  32 large silk ribbon rosebuds (optional)

CUTTING OUT THE PIECES
All measurements include a ¼" seam allowance.
Follow Rotary Cutting, page 16, to cut fabric.

1. **From pink floral:** ☐
   - Cut 5 strips 5¾"w. From these strips, cut 32 **Blocks** 5¾" x 5¾".
2. **From pink solid:** ▨
   - Cut 3 strips 6½"w. From these strips, cut 16 **squares** 6½" x 6½".
3. **From white chenille:** ☐
   - Cut 3 strips 6½"w. From these strips, cut 16 **squares** 6½" x 6½".

ASSEMBLING THE QUILT TOP
Follow Piecing and Pressing, page 19, to make quilt top.

1. On wrong side of each pink solid **square**, draw diagonal lines from corner to corner in both directions.
2. Place 1 pink solid **square** and 1 white chenille **square** right sides together. Stitch seam ¼" on each side of 1 drawn line (**Fig. 1**). Press stitching. Cut apart along drawn line (**Fig. 2**) to make 2 triangle-squares. Press triangle-squares open (**Fig. 3**).

Fig. 1   Fig. 2   Fig. 3

3. On wrong side of 1 triangle-square, extend drawn line from corner of pink solid triangle to corner of white chenille triangle.

4. Match both triangle-squares with contrasting fabrics facing and marked unit on top. Stitch seam ¼" on each side of drawn line (**Fig. 4**). Cut apart along drawn line (**Fig. 5**) to make 2 **Hourglass Blocks**. Press **Hourglass Blocks** open.

Fig. 4   Fig. 5   Hourglass Blocks

5. Repeat Steps 1 – 4 to make 32 **Hourglass Blocks**.
6. Referring to photo, sew 4 **Hourglass Blocks** and 4 pink floral **Blocks** together to make 1 **Row**. Make 8 **Rows**. Sew **Rows** together to make quilt top.

COMPLETING THE QUILT
1. Follow **Quilting**, page 21, to mark, layer and quilt as desired. Our quilt is machine quilted "in the ditch". Sew silk roses in the center of each **Hourglass Block** if desired.
   ***NOTE:** Small objects can be a choking hazard for babies or small children. Make sure they are securely attached.*
2. Cut a 23" square of binding fabric. Follow **Binding**, page 25, to bind quilt using 2½"w bias binding with mitered corners.

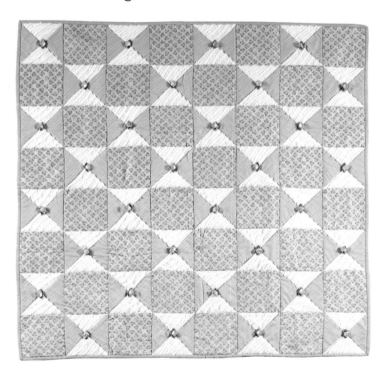

Toy Boats

If naptime becomes fussy time, wrap your little one in this comfy quilt and soothe away those baby blues! Triangle-squares — formed from blue flannel print and white chenille — are set in the same direction, creating an illusion of sails blowing in the wind. A border of simple stripes adds to the quilt's shipshape design.

Block Size: 5¹⁄₈" x 5¹⁄₈" (13 x 13 cm)
Quilt Size: 46³⁄₄" x 46³⁄₄" (119 cm x 119 cm)

YARDAGE REQUIREMENTS

Yardage is based on 45"w fabric. For all fabrics other than the chenille, we used flannel.

- 1¹⁄₄ yd (1.1 m) blue stripe
- 1³⁄₈ yd (1.3 m) blue print
- 1¹⁄₂ yd (1.4 m) white chenille
  3 yds (2.7 m) for backing
  ³⁄₄ yd (69 cm) for binding
  51" x 51" (130 x 130 cm) square of batting

CUTTING OUT THE PIECES

All measurements include a ¹⁄₄" seam allowance. Follow Rotary Cutting, page 16, to cut fabric.

1. **From blue stripe:**
   - Cut 2 lengthwise **top/bottom inner borders** 40¹⁄₄" x 4".
   - Cut 2 lengthwise **side inner borders** 33¹⁄₄" x 4".

2. **From blue print:**
   - Cut 2 lengthwise **top/bottom middle borders** 43¹⁄₄" x 2".
   - Cut 2 lengthwise **side middle borders** 40¹⁄₄" x 2".
   - From remaining fabric width, cut 4 strips 6"w. From these strips, cut 18 **squares** 6" x 6".

3. **From white chenille:** ☐
   - Cut 2 lengthwise **top/bottom outer borders** 48¹⁄₄" x 3".
   - Cut 2 lengthwise **side outer borders** 43¹⁄₄" x 3".
   - From remaining fabric width, cut 5 strips 6"w. From these strips, cut 18 **squares** 6" x 6".

ASSEMBLING THE QUILT TOP

Follow Piecing and Pressing, page 19, to make quilt top.

1. Draw line diagonally (corner to corner) on wrong side of each blue print square.

2. Place 1 blue print square and 1 white chenille square right sides together. Stitch seam ¹⁄₄" on each side of drawn line (**Fig. 1**). Repeat with remaining **squares**.

Fig. 1

3. Cut drawn line. Press open to make 2 **Blocks** (triangle-squares). Repeat to make 36 **Blocks**.

Fig. 2   Blocks (Make 36)

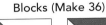

4. Referring to photo, sew 6 **Blocks** together to make **Row**. Make 6 **Rows**. Sew **Rows** together to make center section of quilt top.

5. Follow **Adding Squared Borders**, page 20, to add **side**, then **top and bottom inner borders** to center section of quilt top. Repeat to add **middle** and **outer borders** to complete quilt top.

COMPLETING THE QUILT

1. Follow **Quilting**, page 21, to mark, layer and quilt as desired. Our quilt is machine quilted "in the ditch".

2. Cut a 24" square of binding fabric. Follow **Binding**, page 25, to bind quilt using 2¹⁄₂"w bias binding with mitered corners.

7

Pastel Squares

This all-chenille quilt offers the ultimate in cuddly comfort! An assortment of pastel chenille scraps make up the soft and fluffy design. The touch-tempting texture will entice tiny tots to explore a variety of patterns, such as lines, dots, swirls, and flowers. We tied our quilt at the corner of each square for a fast finish.

Block Size: 4³/₄" x 4³/₄" (12 x 12 cm)
Quilt Size: 43³/₄" x 43³/₄" (111 x 111 cm)

YARDAGE REQUIREMENTS

 ¹/₄ yd (23 cm) each of 12 assorted chenille fabrics

3 yds (2.7 m) flannel or other fabric for backing

³/₄ yd (69 cm) for binding

48" x 48" (122 x 122 cm) square high loft bonded batting

15 yds (13.7 m) of ¹/₈" (3 mm) ribbon or yarn for tying

CUTTING OUT THE PIECES

All measurements include a ¹/₄" seam allowance. Follow **Rotary Cutting**, *page 16, to cut fabric.*

1. From assorted chenille fabrics:

- Cut 1 strip 5¹/₄"w from each fabric. From strips, cut **squares** 5¹/₄" x 5¹/₄", for a total of 81 **squares**.

ASSEMBLING THE QUILT TOP

Follow **Piecing and Pressing**, *page 19, to make quilt top.*

1. Arrange all **squares** on flat surface into 9 **Rows** of 9 **squares** each. Refer to photo for placement example.
2. Sew 9 **squares** together to make 1 **Row**. Make 9 **Rows**.
3. Sew 9 **Rows** together to make quilt top.

COMPLETING THE QUILT

1. Layer backing (right side down), batting, and quilt top (right side up). Pin layers together with safety pins or stretch on quilting frame.
2. Follow **Tying a Quilt**, page 24, to tie quilt with 1 strand of ¹/₈" ribbon or yarn. Our quilt was tied at each corner of squares with white satin ribbon.
3. Cut a 23" square of binding fabric. Follow **Binding**, page 25, to bind quilt using 2¹/₂"w bias binding with mitered corners.

Building Blocks

Babies have so much fun playing with blocks that they don't even realize they're learning, too. Spark your little one's interest with this fun yet simple building blocks quilt. Bold Four-Patch blocks — pieced from red chenille and blue print — are set with plaid squares and machine stipple quilted to create the striking design.

Block Size: 8" x 8" (20 x 20 cm)
Quilt Size: 41" x 41" (104 x 104 cm)

YARDAGE REQUIREMENTS
Yardage is based on 45"w fabric.

- ◼ 1/2 yd (46 cm) red chenille
- ◼ 1/2 yd (46 cm) blue print
- ☐ 7/8 yd (80 cm) white plaid
  1 3/8 yds (1.3 m) for backing
  3/4 yd (69 cm) for binding
  45"x 45" (114 x 114 cm) square batting

CUTTING OUT THE PIECES
All measurements include a 1/4" seam allowance.
Follow Rotary Cutting, page 16, to cut fabric.

1. **From red chenille:** ◼
   - Cut 3 strips 4 1/2"w. From strips, cut 26 **small squares** 4 1/2" x 4 1/2".
2. **From blue print:** ◼
   - Cut 3 strips 4 1/2"w. From strips, cut 26 **small squares** 4 1/2" x 4 1/2".
3. **From white plaid:** ☐
   - Cut 3 strips 8 1/2"w. From strips, cut 12 **large squares** 8 1/2" x 8 1/2".

ASSEMBLING THE QUILT TOP
Follow Piecing and Pressing, page 19, to make quilt top.

1. Sew 2 red chenille **small squares** and 2 blue print **small squares** together to make **Four-Patch Block**. Make 13 **Four-Patch Blocks**.

Four-Patch Block (make 13)

2. Sew 3 **Four-Patch Blocks** and 2 **large squares** together to make **Row A**. Make 3 **Row A's**.

Row A (make 3)

3. Sew 2 **Four-Patch Blocks** and 3 **large squares** together to make **Row B**. Make 2 **Row B's**.

Row B (make 2)

4. Referring to photo, sew **Rows** together to make quilt top.

COMPLETING THE QUILT

1. Follow **Quilting**, page 21, to mark, layer and quilt as desired. Our quilt is machine stipple quilted.
2. Cut a 23" square of binding fabric. Follow **Binding**, page 25, to bind quilt using 2 1/2"w bias binding with mitered corners.

Red & Blue Pinwheels

Giving the illusion of pinwheels spinning in the breeze, this quilt is sure to delight Baby! A perky polka-dot print is paired with both blue and red chenille to make triangle-squares, which are arranged to produce the pinwheel pattern. Machine stipple quilting lends childlike whimsy to the quilt.

BLOCK SIZE: 7 1/8" x 7 1/8" (18 x 18 cm)
QUILT SIZE: 43 3/4" x 43 3/4" (111 x 111 cm)

YARDAGE REQUIREMENTS

Yardage is based on 45"w fabric.

- 1/2 yd (46 cm) blue chenille
- 1/2 yd (46 cm) red chenille
- 1 yd (91 cm) white print
  3 yds (2.7 m) for backing
  3/4 yd (69 cm) for binding
  48" x 48" (122 x 122 cm) square of batting

CUTTING OUT THE PIECES

All measurements include a 1/4" seam allowance.
Follow Rotary Cutting, page 16, to cut fabric.

1. **From blue chenille:**
    - Cut 2 strips 8"w. From these strips, cut 9 **squares**, 8" x 8".
2. **From red chenille:**
    - Cut 2 strips 8"w. From these strips, cut 9 **squares**, 8" x 8".
3. **From white print:**
    - Cut 4 strips 8"w. From these strips, cut 18 **squares**, 8" x 8".

ASSEMBLING THE QUILT TOP

Follow Piecing and Pressing, page 19, to make quilt top.

1. Draw line diagonally (corner to corner) on wrong side of each white print **square**.
2. Place 1 white print **square** and one chenille **square** right sides together. Stitch seam 1/4" on each side of drawn line (**Fig. 1**). Repeat with remaining **squares**.

Fig. 1

3. Cut drawn line to make 2 **Blocks** (triangle-squares). Repeat to make 18 **Blocks** with blue chenille and 18 **Blocks** with red chenille.

Blocks (make 18 red and 18 blue)

4. Referring to photo for placement, sew 6 **Blocks** together to make **Row**. Make 5 **Rows**. Sew **Rows** together to make quilt top.

COMPLETING THE QUILT

1. Follow **Quilting**, page 21, to mark, layer and quilt as desired. Our quilt is machine stipple quilted.
2. Cut a 23" square of binding fabric. Follow **Binding**, page 25, to bind quilt using 2 1/2"w bias binding with mitered corners.

General Instructions

Complete instructions are given for making each of the projects shown in this book. To make your quilting easier and more enjoyable, we encourage you to carefully read all of the general instructions, study the color photographs, and familiarize yourself with the individual project instructions before beginning a project.

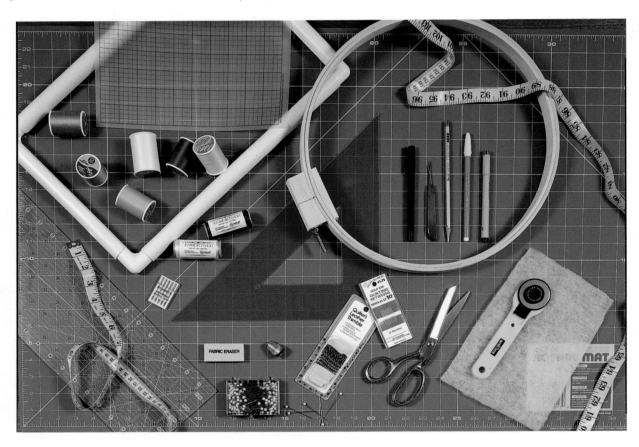

QUILTING SUPPLIES

This list includes all the tools you need for basic quick-method quiltmaking, plus additional supplies used for special techniques. Unless otherwise specified, all items may be found in your favorite fabric store or quilt shop.

Batting — Batting is most commonly available in polyester, cotton, or a polyester/cotton blend (see **Choosing and Preparing the Batting**, page 22).

Cutting mat — A cutting mat is a special mat designed to be used with a rotary cutter. A mat that measures approximately 18" x 24" is a good size for most cutting.

Eraser — A soft white fabric eraser or white art eraser may be used to remove pencil marks from fabric. Do not use a colored eraser, as the dye may discolor fabric.

Iron — An iron with both steam and dry settings and a smooth, clean soleplate is necessary for proper pressing.

Marking tools — There are many different marking tools available (see **Marking Quilting Lines**, page 21). A silver quilter's pencil is a good marker for both light and dark fabrics.

Masking tape — Two widths of masking tape, 1"w and 1/4"w, are helpful when quilting. The 1"w tape is used to secure the backing fabric to a flat surface when layering the quilt. The 1/4"w tape may be used as a guide when outline quilting.

Needles — Two types of needles are used for hand sewing: Betweens, used for quilting, are short and strong for stitching through layered fabric and batting. Sharps are longer, thinner needles used for basting and other hand sewing. For sewing machine needles, we recommend size 10 to 14 or 70 to 90 universal (sharp-pointed) needles.

Permanent fine-point pen — A permanent pen is used to mark templates and stencils and to sign and date quilts. Test pen on fabric to make sure it will not bleed or wash out.

Pins — Straight pins made especially for quilting are extra long with large round heads. Glass head pins will stand up to occasional contact with a hot iron. Some quilters prefer extra-fine dressmaker's silk pins. If you are machine quilting, you will need a large supply of 1" long (size 01) rustproof safety pins for pin-basting.

Quilting hoop or frame — Quilting hoops and frames are designed to hold the 3 layers of a quilt together securely while you quilt. Many different types and sizes are available, including round and oval wooden hoops, frames made of rigid plastic pipe, and large floor frames made of either material. A 14" or 16" hoop allows you to quilt in your lap and makes your quilting portable.

Rotary cutter — The rotary cutter is the essential tool for quick-method quilting techniques. The cutter consists of a round, sharp blade mounted on a handle with a retractable blade guard for safety. It should be used only with a cutting mat and rotary cutting ruler. Different sizes are available; we recommend the 45 mm size.

Rotary cutting ruler — A rotary cutting ruler is a thick, clear acrylic ruler made specifically for use with a rotary cutter. It should have accurate 1/8" crosswise and lengthwise markings and markings for 45° and 60° angles. A 6" x 24" ruler is a good size for most cutting. An additional 6" x 12" ruler or 12 1/2" square ruler is helpful when cutting wider pieces. Many specialty rulers are available that make specific cutting tasks faster and easier.

Scissors — Although most fabric cutting will be done with a rotary cutter, sharp, high-quality scissors are still needed for some cutting. A separate pair of scissors for cutting paper and plastic is recommended. Smaller scissors are handy for clipping threads.

Seam ripper — A good seam ripper with a fine point is useful for removing stitching.

Sewing machine — A sewing machine that produces a good, even straight stitch is all that is necessary for most quilting. Clean and oil your machine often and keep the tension set properly.

Tape measure — A flexible 120" long tape measure is helpful for measuring a quilt top before adding borders.

Template material — Sheets of translucent plastic, often pre-marked with a grid, are made especially for making quilting stencils.

Thimble — A thimble is necessary when hand quilting. Thimbles are available in metal, plastic, or leather and in many sizes and styles. Choose a thimble that fits well and is comfortable.

Thread — Several types of thread are used for quiltmaking: General-purpose sewing thread is used for basting and piecing. Choose high-quality cotton or cotton-covered polyester thread in light and dark neutrals, such as ecru and grey, for your basic supplies. Quilting thread is stronger than general-purpose sewing thread, and some brands have a coating to make them slide more easily through the quilt layers.

Triangle — A large plastic right-angle triangle (available in art and office supply stores) is useful in rotary cutting for making first cuts to "square up" raw edges of fabric and for checking to see that cuts remain at right angles to the fold.

Walking foot — A walking foot, or even-feed foot, is needed for straight-line machine quilting. This special foot will help all 3 layers move at the same rate over the feed dogs to provide a smoother quilted project.

FABRICS

SELECTING FABRICS

Choose high-quality, medium-weight 100% cotton fabrics such as broadcloth or calico. All-cotton fabrics hold a crease better, fray less, and are easier to quilt than cotton/polyester blends. All the fabrics for a quilt should be of comparable weight and weave. Check the end of the fabric bolt for fiber content and width.

The yardage requirements listed for each project are based on 45" wide fabric with a "usable" width of 42" after shrinkage and trimming selvages. Your actual usable width will probably vary slightly from fabric to fabric. Though most fabrics will yield 42" or more, if you find a fabric that you suspect will yield a narrower usable width, you will need to purchase additional yardage to compensate. Our recommended yardage lengths should be adequate for occasional re-squaring of fabric when many cuts are required, but it never hurts to buy a little more fabric for insurance against a narrower usable width, the occasional cutting error, or to have on hand for making coordinating projects.

PREPARING FABRICS

All fabrics should be washed, dried, and pressed before cutting.

1. To check colorfastness before washing, cut a small piece of the fabric and place in a glass of hot water with a little detergent. Leave fabric in the water for a few minutes. Remove fabric from water and blot with white paper towels. If any color bleeds onto the towels, wash the fabric separately with warm water and detergent, then rinse until the water runs clear. If fabric continues to bleed, choose another fabric.

2. Unfold yardage and separate fabrics by color. To help reduce raveling, use scissors to snip a small triangle from each corner of your fabric pieces. Machine wash fabrics in warm water with a small amount of mild laundry detergent. Do not use fabric softener. Rinse well and then dry fabrics in the dryer, checking long fabric lengths occasionally to make sure they are not tangling.

3. To make ironing easier, remove fabrics from dryer while they are slightly damp. Refold each fabric lengthwise (as it was on the bolt) with wrong sides together and matching selvages. If necessary, adjust slightly at selvages so that fold lays flat. Press each fabric using a steam iron set on "Cotton."

ROTARY CUTTING

*Based on the idea that you can easily cut strips of fabric and then cut those strips into smaller pieces, rotary cutting has brought speed and accuracy to quiltmaking. Observe safety precautions when using the rotary cutter, since it is extremely sharp. Develop a habit of retracting the blade guard **just before** making a cut and closing it **immediately afterward,** before laying down the cutter.*

1. Follow **Preparing Fabrics** to wash, dry, and press fabrics.

2. Cut all strips from the selvage-to-selvage width of the fabric unless otherwise indicated in project instructions. Place fabric on the cutting mat, as shown in **Fig. 1**, with the fold of the fabric toward you. To straighten the uneven fabric edge, make the first "squaring up" cut by placing the right edge of the rotary cutting ruler over the left raw edge of the fabric. Place right-angle triangle (or another rotary cutting ruler) with the lower edge carefully aligned with the fold and the left edge against the ruler (**Fig. 1**). Hold the ruler firmly with your left hand, placing your little finger off the left edge to anchor the ruler.

Remove the triangle, pick up the rotary cutter, and retract the blade guard. Using a smooth downward motion, make the cut by running the blade of the rotary cutter firmly along the right edge of the ruler (**Fig. 2**). **Always** cut in a direction **away** from your body and **immediately** close the blade guard after each cut.

Fig. 1   Fig. 2

3. To cut each of the strips required for a project, place the ruler over the cut edge of the fabric, aligning desired marking on the ruler with the cut edge (**Fig. 3**); make the cut. When cutting several strips from a single piece of fabric, it is important to occasionally use the ruler and triangle to ensure that cuts are still at a perfect right angle to the fold. If not, repeat Step 2 to straighten.

Fig. 3

4. To square up selvage ends of a strip before cutting pieces, refer to **Fig. 4** and place folded strip on mat with selvage ends to your right. Aligning a horizontal marking on ruler with 1 long edge of strip, use rotary cutter to trim selvage to make end of strip square and even (**Fig. 4**). Turn strip (or entire mat) so that cut end is to your left before making subsequent cuts.

Fig. 4

5. Pieces such as rectangles and squares can now be cut from strips. Usually strips remain folded, and pieces are cut in pairs after ends of strips are squared up. To cut squares or rectangles from a strip, place ruler over left end of strip, aligning desired marking on ruler with cut end of strip. To ensure perfectly square cuts, align a horizontal marking on ruler with 1 long edge of strip (**Fig. 5**) before making the cut.

Fig. 5

6. To cut 2 triangles from a square, cut square the size indicated in the project instructions. Cut square once diagonally to make 2 triangles (**Fig. 6**).

Fig. 6

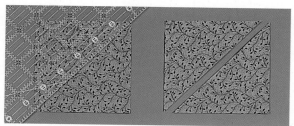

7. To cut 4 triangles from a square, cut square the size indicated in the project instructions. Cut square twice diagonally to make 4 triangles (**Fig. 7**). You may find it helpful to use a small rotary cutting mat so that the mat can be turned to make second cut without disturbing fabric pieces.

Fig. 7

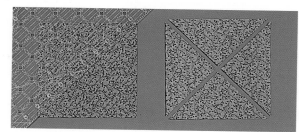

8. After some practice, you may want to try stacking up to 6 fabric layers when making cuts. When stacking strips, match long cut edges and follow Step 4 to square up ends of strip stack. Carefully turn stack (or entire mat) so that squared-up ends are to your left before making subsequent cuts. After cutting, check accuracy of pieces. Some shapes, such as diamonds, are more difficult to cut accurately in stacks.

9. In some cases, strips will be sewn together into strip sets before being cut into smaller units. When cutting a strip set, align a seam in strip set with a horizontal marking on the ruler to maintain square cuts (**Fig. 8**). We do not recommend stacking strip sets for rotary cutting.

Fig. 8

10. Most borders for quilts in this book are cut along the more stable lengthwise grain to minimize wavy edges caused by stretching. To remove selvages before cutting lengthwise strips, place fabric on mat with selvages to your left and squared-up end at bottom of mat. Placing ruler over selvage and using squared-up edge instead of fold, follow Step 2 to cut away selvages as you did raw edges (**Fig. 9**). After making a cut the length of the mat, move the next section of fabric to be cut onto the mat. Repeat until you have removed selvages from required length of fabric.

Fig. 9

11. After removing selvages, place ruler over left edge of fabric, aligning desired marking on ruler with cut edge of fabric. Make cuts as in Step 3. After each cut, move next section of fabric onto mat as in Step 10.

PIECING AND PRESSING

Precise cutting, followed by accurate piecing and careful pressing, will ensure that all the pieces of your quilt top fit together well.

PIECING

Set sewing machine stitch length for approximately 11 stitches per inch. Use a new, sharp needle suited for medium-weight woven fabric.

Use a neutral-colored general-purpose sewing thread (not quilting thread) in the needle and in the bobbin. Stitch first on a scrap of fabric to check upper and bobbin thread tension; make any adjustments necessary.

For good results, it is **essential** that you stitch with an **accurate** 1/4" **seam allowance**. On many sewing machines, the measurement from the needle to the outer edge of the presser foot is 1/4". If this is the case with your machine, the presser foot is your best guide. If not, measure 1/4" from the needle and mark throat plate with a piece of masking tape. Special presser feet that are exactly 1/4" wide are also available for most sewing machines.

When piecing, **always** place pieces **right sides together** and **match raw edges**; pin if necessary. (If using straight pins, remove the pins just before they reach the sewing machine needle.)

Chain Piecing

Chain piecing whenever possible will make your work go faster and will usually result in more accurate piecing. Stack the pieces you will be sewing beside your machine in the order you will need them and in a position that will allow you to easily pick them up. Pick up each pair of pieces, carefully place them together as they will be sewn, and feed them into the machine one after the other. Stop between each pair only long enough to pick up the next pair; don't cut thread between pairs (**Fig. 10**). After all pieces are sewn, cut threads, press, and go on to the next step, chain piecing when possible.

Fig. 10

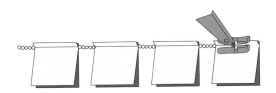

Sewing Across Seam Intersections

When sewing across the intersection of 2 seams, place pieces right sides together and match seams exactly, making sure seam allowances are pressed in opposite directions (**Fig. 11**). To prevent fabric from shifting, you may wish to pin in place.

Fig. 11

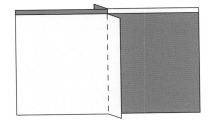

Sewing Bias Seams

Care should be used in handling and stitching bias edges since they stretch easily. After sewing the seam, carefully press seam allowance to 1 side, making sure not to stretch fabric.

Sewing Sharp Points

To ensure sharp points when joining triangular or diagonal pieces, stitch across the center of the "X" (shown in pink) formed on the wrong side by previous seams (**Fig. 12**).

Fig. 12

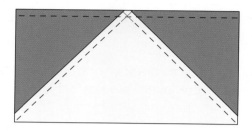

Trimming Seam Allowances

When sewing with triangle pieces, some seam allowances may extend beyond the edges of the sewn pieces. Trim away "dog ears" that extend beyond the edges of the sewn pieces (**Fig. 13**).

Fig. 13

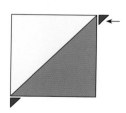

Pressing

Use a steam iron set on "Cotton" for all pressing. Press as you sew, taking care to prevent small folds along seamlines. Seam allowances are almost always pressed to one side, usually toward the darker fabric. However, to reduce bulk it may occasionally be necessary to press seam allowances toward the lighter fabric or even to press them open. In order to prevent a dark fabric seam allowance from showing through a light fabric, trim the darker seam allowance slightly narrower than the lighter seam allowance. To press long seams, such as those in long strip sets, without curving or other distortion, lay strips across the width of the ironing board.

BORDERS

Borders cut along the lengthwise grain will lie flatter than borders cut along the crosswise grain. Our instructions for cutting borders for the baby quilts include an extra 1" of length at each end for "insurance"; borders will be trimmed after measuring completed center section of quilt top.

ADDING SQUARED BORDERS

1. Mark the center of each edge of quilt top.
2. To add side borders, measure down center of quilt top to determine length of borders (**Fig. 14**). Trim side borders to the determined length.

Fig. 14

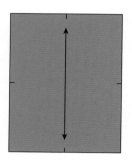

3. Mark center of 1 long edge of side border. Matching center marks and raw edges, pin border to quilt top, easing in any fullness; stitch. Repeat for other side border.
4. Measure center of quilt top, including attached borders, to determine length of top and bottom borders. Trim top and bottom borders to the determined length. Repeat Step 3 to add borders to quilt top (**Fig. 15**).

Fig. 15

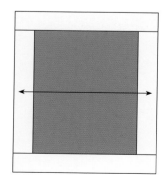

QUILTING

Quilting holds the 3 layers (top, batting, and backing) of the quilt together and can be done by hand or machine.

TYPES OF QUILTING

In the Ditch

Quilting very close to a seamline (**Fig. 16**) or appliqué (**Fig. 17**) is called "in the ditch" quilting and does not need to be marked. When quilting in the ditch, quilt on the side **opposite** the seam allowance.

Fig. 16

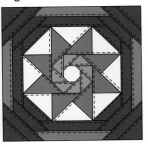

Fig. 17

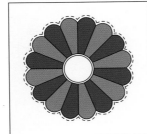

Outline Quilting

Quilting approximately ¼" from a seam or appliqué is called "outline" quilting (**Fig. 18**). Outline quilting may be marked, or you may place ¼"w masking tape along seamlines and quilt along the opposite edge of the tape. (Do not leave tape on quilt longer than necessary, since it may leave an adhesive residue.)

Fig. 18

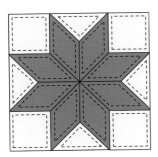

MARKING QUILTING LINES

Fabric marking pencils, various types of chalk markers, and fabric marking pens with inks that disappear with exposure to air or water are readily available and work well for different applications. Lead pencils work well on light-color fabrics, but marks may be difficult to remove. White pencils work well on dark-color fabrics, and silver pencils show up well on many colors. Since chalk rubs off easily, it's a good choice if you are marking as you quilt. Fabric marking pens make more durable and visible markings, but the marks should be carefully removed according to manufacturer's instructions. Press down only as hard as necessary to make a visible line.

When you choose to mark your quilt, whether before or after the layers are basted together, is also a factor in deciding which marking tool to use. If you mark with chalk or a chalk pencil, handling the quilt during basting may rub off the markings. Intricate or ornamental designs may not be practical to mark as you quilt; mark these designs before basting using a more durable marker.

To choose marking tools, take all these factors into consideration and **test** different markers **on scrap fabric** until you find the one that gives the desired result.

CHOOSING AND PREPARING THE BACKING

To allow for slight shifting of the quilt top during quilting, the backing should be approximately 2" larger on all sides for a baby-size quilt top. Yardage requirements listed for quilt backings are calculated for 45"w fabric, and 1 width may be sufficient. If not, piece a backing using the following instructions.

1.   Measure length and width of quilt top; add 4" to each measurement.
2.   Cut backing fabric into 2 lengths slightly longer than the determined **length** measurement. Trim selvages. Place lengths with right sides facing and sew long edges together, forming a tube (**Fig. 19**). Match seams and press along 1 fold (**Fig. 20**). Cut along pressed fold to form a single piece (**Fig. 21**).

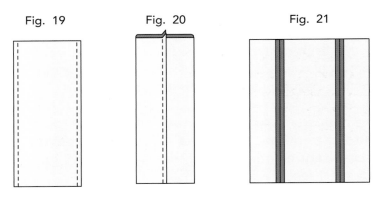

| Fig. 19 | Fig. 20 | Fig. 21 |

3.   Trim backing to correct size, if necessary, and press seam allowances open.

CHOOSING AND PREPARING THE BATTING

Choosing the right batting will make your quilting job easier. For fine hand quilting, choose a low-loft batting in any of the fiber types described here. Machine quilters will want to choose a low-loft batting that is all cotton or a cotton/polyester blend because the cotton helps "grip" the layers of the quilt. If the quilt is to be tied, a high-loft batting, sometimes called extra-loft or fat batting, is a good choice.

Batting is available in many different fibers. Bonded polyester batting is one of the most popular batting types. It is treated with a protective coating to stabilize the fibers and to reduce "bearding," a process in which batting fibers work their way out through the quilt fabrics. Other batting options include cotton/polyester batting, which combines the best of both polyester and cotton battings; all-cotton batting, which must be quilted more closely than polyester batting; and wool and silk battings, which are generally more expensive and usually only dry-cleanable.

Whichever batting you choose, read the manufacturer's instructions closely for any special notes on care or preparation. When you're ready to use your chosen batting in a project, cut batting the same size as the prepared backing.

ASSEMBLING THE QUILT

1.   Examine wrong side of quilt top closely; trim any seam allowances and clip any threads that may show through the front of the quilt. Press quilt top.
2.   If quilt top is to be marked before layering, mark quilting lines (see **Marking Quilting Lines**, page 21).
3.   Place backing **wrong** side up on a flat surface. Use masking tape to tape edges of backing to surface. Place batting on top of backing fabric. Smooth batting gently, being careful not to stretch or tear. Center quilt top **right** side up on batting.
4.   If hand quilting, begin in the center and work toward the outer edges to hand baste all layers together. Use long stitches and place basting lines approximately 4" apart (**Fig. 22**). Smooth fullness or wrinkles toward outer edges.

Fig. 22

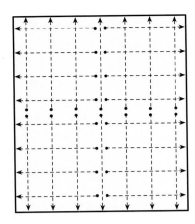

Fig. 23

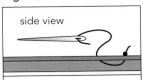

Fig. 24

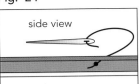

5. If machine quilting, use 1" rustproof safety pins to "pin-baste" all layers together, spacing pins approximately 4" apart. Begin at the center and work toward the outer edges to secure all layers. If possible, place pins away from areas that will be quilted, although pins may be removed as needed when quilting.

HAND QUILTING

The quilting stitch is a basic running stitch that forms a broken line on the quilt top and backing. Stitches on the quilt top and backing should be straight and equal in length.

1. Secure center of quilt in hoop or frame. Check quilt top and backing to make sure they are smooth. To help prevent puckers, always begin quilting in the center of the quilt and work toward the outside edges.

2. Thread needle with an 18" - 20" length of quilting thread; knot 1 end. Using a thimble, insert needle into quilt top and batting approximately 1/2" from where you wish to begin quilting. Bring needle up at the point where you wish to begin (**Fig. 23**); when knot catches on quilt top, give thread a quick, short pull to "pop" knot through fabric into batting (**Fig. 24**).

3. Holding the needle with your sewing hand and placing your other hand underneath the quilt, use thimble to push the tip of the needle down through all layers. As soon as needle touches your finger underneath, use that finger to push the tip of the needle only back up through the layers to top of quilt. (The amount of the needle showing above the fabric determines the length of the quilting stitch.) Referring to **Fig. 25**, rock the needle up and down, taking 3 - 6 stitches before bringing the needle and thread completely through the layers. Check the back of the quilt to make sure stitches are going through all layers. When quilting through a seam allowance or quilting a curve or corner, you may need to make 1 stitch at a time.

Fig. 25

4. When you reach the end of your thread, knot thread close to the fabric and "pop" knot into batting; clip thread close to fabric.

5. Stop and move your hoop as often as necessary. You do not have to tie a knot every time you move your hoop; you may leave the thread dangling and pick it up again when you return to that part of the quilt.

MACHINE QUILTING

The following instructions are for straight-line quilting, which requires a walking foot or even-feed foot. The term "straight-line" is somewhat deceptive, since curves (especially gentle ones) as well as straight lines can be stitched with this technique.

1. Wind your sewing machine bobbin with general-purpose thread that matches the quilt backing. Do not use quilting thread. Thread the needle of your machine with transparent monofilament thread if you want your quilting to blend with your quilt top fabrics. Use decorative thread, such as a metallic or contrasting-color general-purpose thread, when you want the quilting lines to stand out more. Set the stitch length for 6 - 10 stitches per inch and attach the walking foot to sewing machine.

2. After pin-basting, decide which section of the quilt will have the longest continuous quilting line, oftentimes the area from center top to center bottom. Leaving the area exposed where you will place your first line of quilting, roll up each edge of the quilt to help reduce the bulk, keeping fabrics smooth. Smaller projects may not need to be rolled.

3. Start stitching at beginning of longest quilting line, using very short stitches for the first ¼" to "lock" beginning of quilting line. Stitch across project, using one hand on each side of the walking foot to slightly spread the fabric and to guide the fabric through the machine. Lock stitches at end of quilting line.

4. Continue machine quilting, stitching longer quilting lines first to stabilize the quilt before moving on to other areas.

MACHINE STIPPLE QUILTING

The term, "stipple quilting," refers to dense quilting using a meandering line of machine stitching or closely spaced hand stitching.

1. For random stipple quilting, use a darning foot, drop or cover feed dogs, and set stitch length at zero. Pull up bobbin thread and hold both thread ends while you stitch 2 or 3 stitches in place to lock thread. Cut threads near quilt surface. Place hands lightly on quilt on either side of darning foot.

2. Begin stitching in a meandering pattern (**Fig. 26**), guiding the quilt with your hands. The object is to make stitches of similar length and to not sew over previous stitching lines. The movement of your hands is what determines the stitch length; it takes practice to coordinate your hand motions and the pressure you put on the foot pedal, so go slowly at first.

Fig. 26

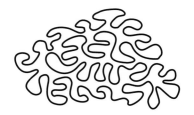

3. Continue machine quilting, filling in one open area of the quilt before moving on to another area, locking thread again at end of each line of stitching by sewing 2 or 3 stitches in place and trimming thread ends.

TYING A QUILT

Tied quilts use ribbon, yarn or floss ties instead of quilting stitches to secure the layers. For a tied quilt, be sure to use bonded batting to prevent separation or bunching when the quilt is laundered. You may also use a higher loft batting than when quilting.

1. Determine where ties will be placed and mark if necessary. Space ties evenly. On a pieced top, tie at corners of blocks or pieces within blocks.

2. Follow **Choosing and Preparing the Backing,** page 22, **Choosing and Preparing the Batting,** page 22, and **Assembling the Quilt,** page 22, to prepare quilt for tying.

3. Thread a large darning needle with a long length of narrow satin ribbon. (You may also use embroidery floss, pearl cotton, or yarn.) Do not knot.

4. At each mark or tie location, take a small stitch through all layers of quilt. Pull up ribbon, but do not cut between stitches (**Fig. 27**). Begin at center of quilt and work toward outside edges, rethreading needle as necessary.

Fig. 27

5. Cut ribbon between stitches. At each stitch, use a square knot to tie ribbon securely (**Fig. 28**); trim ties to desired length.

Fig. 28

BINDING

Binding encloses the raw edges of your quilt. Because of its stretchiness, bias binding works well for binding projects with curves or rounded corners and tends to lie smooth and flat in any given circumstance. It is also more durable than other types of binding.

MAKING CONTINUOUS BIAS STRIP BINDING

Bias strips for binding can simply be cut and pieced to the desired length. However, when a long length of binding is needed, the "continuous" method is quick and accurate.

1. Cut a square from binding fabric the size indicated in the project instructions. Cut square in half diagonally to make 2 triangles.

2. With right sides together and using a 1/4" seam allowance, sew triangles together (**Fig. 29**); press seam allowance open.

Fig. 29

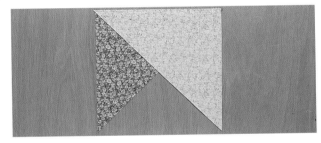

3. On wrong side of fabric, draw lines the width of the binding as specified in the project instructions, usually 2¹/₂" (**Fig. 30**). Cut off any remaining fabric less than this width.

Fig. 30

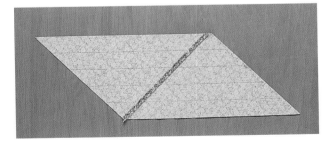

4. With right sides inside, bring short edges together to form a tube; match raw edges so that first drawn line of top section meets second drawn line of bottom section (**Fig. 31**).

Fig. 31

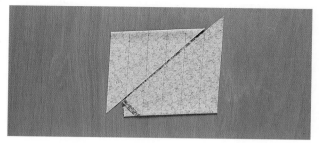

5. Carefully pin edges together by inserting pins through drawn lines at the point where drawn lines intersect, making sure the pins go through intersections on both sides. Using a 1/4" seam allowance, sew edges together. Press seam allowance open.

6. To cut continuous strip, begin cutting along first drawn line (**Fig. 32**). Continue cutting along drawn line around tube.

Fig. 32

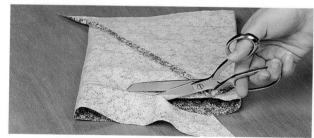

7. Trim ends of bias strip square.

8. Matching wrong sides and raw edges, press bias strip in half lengthwise to complete binding.

ATTACHING BINDING WITH MITERED CORNERS

1. Press 1 end of binding diagonally (**Fig. 33**).

Fig. 33

2. Beginning with pressed end several inches from a corner, lay binding around quilt to make sure that seams in binding will not end up at a corner. Adjust placement if necessary. Matching raw edges of binding to raw edge of quilt top, pin binding to right side of quilt along 1 edge.

3. When you reach the first corner, mark 1/4" from corner of quilt top (**Fig. 34**).

Fig. 34

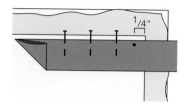

4. Using a 1/4" seam allowance, sew binding to quilt, backstitching at beginning of stitching and when you reach the mark (**Fig. 35**). Lift needle out of fabric and clip thread.

Fig. 35

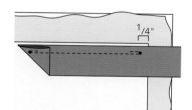

5. Fold binding as shown in **Figs. 36** and **37** and pin binding to adjacent side, matching raw edges. When you reach the next corner, mark ¼" from edge of quilt top.

Fig. 36

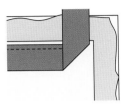

Fig. 37

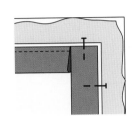

6. Backstitching at edge of quilt top, sew pinned binding to quilt (**Fig. 38**); backstitch when you reach the next mark. Lift needle out of fabric and clip thread.

Fig. 38

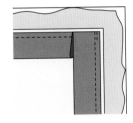

7. Repeat Steps 5 and 6 to continue sewing binding to quilt until binding overlaps beginning end by approximately 2". Trim excess binding.

8. If using 2½"w binding (finished size ½"), trim backing and batting a scant ¼" larger than quilt top so that batting and backing will fill the binding when it is folded over to the quilt backing. If using narrower binding, trim backing and batting even with edges of quilt top.

9. On 1 edge of quilt, fold binding over to quilt backing and pin pressed edge in place, covering stitching line (**Fig. 39**). On adjacent side, fold binding over, forming a mitered corner (**Fig. 40**). Repeat to pin remainder of binding in place.

Fig. 39   Fig. 40

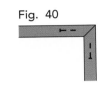

10. Blindstitch (**Fig. 41**) binding to backing, taking care not to stitch through to front of quilt.

Fig. 41

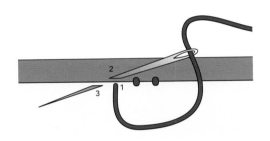

Come up at 1. Go down at 2 and come up at 3. Length of stitches may be varied as desired.

SIGNING AND DATING YOUR QUILT

Your completed quilt is a work of art and should be signed and dated. There are many different ways to do this, and you should pick a method that reflects the style of the quilt, the occasion for which it was made, and your own particular talents.

The following suggestions may give you an idea for recording the history of your quilt for future generations.

- Embroider your name, the date, and any additional information on the quilt top or backing. You may choose embroidery floss colors that closely match the fabric you are working on, such as white floss on a white border, or contrasting colors may be used.
- Make a label from muslin and use a permanent marker to write your information. Your label may be as plain or as fancy as you wish. Stitch the label to the back of the quilt.
- Chart a cross-stitch label design that includes the information you wish and stitch it in colors that complement the quilt. Stitch the finished label to the quilt backing.

Metric Conversion Chart

Inches x 2.54 = centimeters (cm)	Yards x .9144 = meters (m)
Inches x 25.4 = millimeters (mm)	Yards x 91.44 = centimeters (cm)
Inches x .0254 = meters (m)	Centimeters x .3937 = inches (")
	Meters x 1.0936 = yards (yd)

Standard Equivalents

1/8"	3.2 mm	0.32 cm	1/8 yard	11.43 cm	0.11 m
1/4"	6.35 mm	0.635 cm	1/4 yard	22.86 cm	0.23 m
3/8"	9.5 mm	0.95 cm	3/8 yard	34.29 cm	0.34 m
1/2"	12.7 mm	1.27 cm	1/2 yard	45.72 cm	0.46 m
5/8"	15.9 mm	1.59 cm	5/8 yard	57.15 cm	0.57 m
3/4"	19.1 mm	1.91 cm	3/4 yard	68.58 cm	0.69 m
7/8"	22.2 mm	2.22 cm	7/8 yard	80 cm	0.8 m
1"	25.4 mm	2.54 cm	1 yard	91.44 cm	0.91 m

We have made every effort to ensure that these instructions are accurate and complete. We cannot, however, be responsible for human error, typographical mistakes, or variations in individual work.

Production Team: Technical Writer - Frances Huddleston, Editorial Writer - Suzie Puckett, Production Artists - Dayle Cosh and Ashley Carozza, Photography Stylist -Sondra Daniel